T0339775

WELSHMAN HADANE MABHENA: A VOICE FOR MATABELELAND

Marieke Faber Clarke with Pathisa Nyathi

WELSHMAN HADANE MABHENA: A VOICE FOR MATABELELAND

ISBN 978-0-7974-8689-8
EAN 9780797486898

Copyright © Marieke Faber Clarke with Pathisa Nyathi

Published by Amagugu Publishers
Published in 2016

Typeset & designed by Kudzai Chikomo
www.multimediabox.tv

WELSHMAN MABHENA'S FAMILY TREE

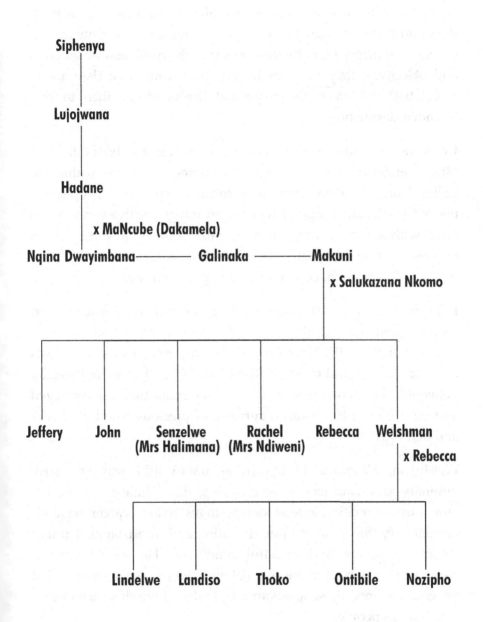

Siphenya

Lujojwana

Hadane

x MaNcube (Dakamela)

Nqina Dwayimbana———— Galinaka ————Makuni

x Salukazana Nkomo

Jeffery   John   Senzelwe   Rachel   Rebecca   Welshman
              (Mrs Halimana) (Mrs Ndiweni)

x Rebecca

Lindelwe   Landiso   Thoko   Ontibile   Nozipho

NOTE FROM THE PUBLISHER

A people without iconic figures are like a radarless ship in pitch dark and turbulent seas. For a people to release the requisite motive energy that drives them forward towards the fulfilment of set goals and objectives, they need clarity on the journey that they are to travel, both in terms of the means and direction to get them to their intended destination.

Iconic figures emerge on several fronts within the broad field of human endeavour. Some emerge as luminous beacons within the political arena. In our case, as a formerly colonized people, we needed inspirational figures that would forego relative comforts on offer within the circumscribed colonial context. Reversal of an oppressive and repressive political system demands men and women of dedication, commitment and perseverance.

Engaging the colonial beast feasting lavishly on instilled fear, coercion and incarceration demands selflessness and unwavering resolve to fight to the bitter end, all the time guided by grand ideals of justice, liberty and freedom. These are values that are not usually delivered like manna from heaven. Quite often they are conveyed and delivered in the crimson currents of precious blood of heroes and heroines.

Welshman, affectionately known as uMawelishi was one such luminary nationalist icon when it came to the relentless fight for the attainment of political independence. In his political career, he faced humiliation, threats to his life, detention and imprisonment under terrible, appalling and dreadful conditions. He served time in various prisons, both in the colonial and independence periods, but never abandoned those ideals that he had set himself to achieve on behalf of his people.

When the lives of such individuals are documented and their experiences brought to the attention of all and sundry, we seek illumination and inspiration that serve as beacons of dedication, commitment, perseverance and unwavering devotion to cherished goals and objectives. For some, it was self-seeking dedication in order to amass pornographic wealth for themselves and their kith and kin in the post-struggle period. Participation in the struggle is then used as an excuse for their unchallenged looting of national resources and unbridled corruption, uncloaked patronage and total denial of the original ideals of the nationalist and armed struggles.

It was not so with Welshman Mabhena. He remained loyal and committed to the ideals that he sacrificed precious time to achieve. When the post-independence long 'moment of madness' came, he stood firm against the mayhem and expressed, without fear, his disgust at such wicked and bloody campaigns by men against fellow men and women. For his views, he was not spared incarceration and battering akin to those inherited from the colonial period. Quite often the past comes back to haunt the present. Our lived colonial experiences revisit us with a vengeance when rulers choose to dwarf colonial oppression and repression. Dissenting voices and non-compliant views are dealt with in a manner more ruthless, vicious and brutal to a point where colonial persecution pales in comparison.

With this publication, it is our hope that it will contribute to the knowledge and lessons about the resistance struggle. While the focus is on an individual, Welshman Mabhena, the search light illuminates the times, both good and bad, that were an integral part of Welshman Mabhena's life. It was a life that stood firmly against the perpetration of evil regardless of who the perpetrator was. This is a value that eludes many when they tolerate the same evil that they took up arms against, only because now the perpetrators' colour is no longer white. Injustice to humankind knows no colour of the perpetrators.

Pathisa Nyathi

Publisher

INTRODUCTION

Welshman Hadane Mabhena, veteran nationalist leader, who served as Governor of Matabeleland North province (1992-2000), became "the godfather for Matabeleland and courted respect from many. He was a true son of the soil whose life he dedicated to serve his own people. He respected fellow human beings, (he was) a favourite of the people and that was why he was affectionately referred to as uMawelishi". [1]

"He was a born leader. You would see that he was from a noble background," said J. Zwelibanzi Mzilethi, who served as his Provincial Administrator (PA).

The Mabhenas did indeed have a long and distinguished history. "The Mabhenas and Mahlangus came together with Mzilikazi(King)," said Garreth Mahlangu, speaking on behalf of Chief Sivalo. "King Lobhengula's Chief Sivalo married a Mabhena woman."

In 1893, Sihuluhulu Mabhena, *induna*[2]of the Emhawini *ibutho* (age-set), was co-commander of the royal bodyguard as British South Africa Company forces pursued the Ndebele King into the dark forests of Matabeleland North.[3] The other bodyguard commander was Sihuluhulu's kinsman Sivalo Mahlangu. These two men were responsible for bringing the king's daughters to safety as the Ndebele kingdom collapsed.[4]

Welshman Mabhena had another well-known heroic kinsman. Under the Ndebele kingdom, Maphungo Mabhena was *induna* of the Umnquma *ibutho*. An *induna* was responsible for the cattle that the king entrusted to him. After the white men's forces occupied

---

[1] Phillip Ndlovu, former Chief Executive Officer, Nkayi Rural District Council.
[2] Commander
[3] Clarke, Marieke, with Nyathi, Pathisa: *"Lozikeyi Dlodlo, Queen of the Ndebele: 'A very dangerous and intriguing woman'"* page 94 and passim; (subsequently 'Clarke and Nyathi')
[4] See Clarke and Nyathi, page 97

7

Matabeleland, A.M. Graham was appointed to be one of their so-called Native Commissioners. The Ndebele called him *uMehlwenduku* or Knobkerry Eyes. Probably in 1895, this cruel man ordered Maphungo Mabhena to hand over the cattle that were in his care.

Mabhena refused to cede the Umnquma animals to Graham. "These cattle are in my custody," he said. Graham then ordered his policemen to tie up Maphungo Mabhena. The *induna* was dragged behind fast-moving horses in hilly country so that his head was crushed.[5]

In 1896, inspired by King Lobhengula's senior wife and Queen Regent, Lozikeyi Dlodlo, the Ndebele people rose in revolt. Sihuluhulu Mabhena fought in that War[6] which in 1896 almost succeeded in driving the white settlers out of Matabeleland.

From 1888 to 1918, Rev. Bowen Rees was the London Missionary Society (LMS) worker at Inyathi Mission in the heart of Ndebele country.[7] He had certainly deeply respected, and told his family he loved, King Lobhengula.[8] Rees himself was much respected by the Ndebele, traumatised by the loss of their king and country. They called him uLesi.

In 1909, the Queen Regent (in a peremptory tone)[9] asked Rees to send his most distinguished convert, Mathambo Ndlovu, to be chaplain at her court. The queen wanted the white men's education for her people. Mathambo was distantly related by marriage to the Mabhenas: his daughter was married to Masotsha, a son of Chief

---

5 Welshman Mabhena, personal communication
6 Pathisa Nyathi in Sunday News, Imfazo 11 Article J, 1996
7 For detailed information about religious developments in Matabeleland North after 1909, see Clarke and Nyathi: Chapter 7.
8 Ioan Bowen Rees, pers. comm
9 Mahlangu (Mrs Amos Mzilethi) smilingly told the present writer how the queen effectively ordered Rev Rees to send Mathambo Ndlovu to her court. Sadly, every effort to find the precious letter she sent has failed.

Sivalo Mahlangu.[10]Also in 1909, Chief Sihuluhulu Mabhena asked Rev. Bowen Rees to open schools in his area.

While Queen Lozikeyi Dlodlo was Queen Regent, the LMS became a sort of "Religion by appointment" to the Royal Family. While Mathambo Ndlovu led Christian services at the Queen's Ranch, [11]traditional Zulu religious ceremonies were still held there. Meanwhile, the indigenous Mwali Religion was greatly respected. [12]The three religions co-existed in harmony.

In 1918 Rev. Bowen Rees retired and left Inyathi Mission to work at Tiger Kloof, the famous LMS higher education institution in South Africa. He returned for a last visit to Matabeleland in 1919. On that trip he baptised Welshman Mabhena.[13]

For Chief Sihuluhulu Mabhena had a brother, Hadane who, under the Kingdom, lived in Matabeleland South. Hadane Mabhena fathered a son, Makuni. As white men occupied the best land in Matabeleland, the adult Makuni was forced to move north, away from the fertile heartlands. At first he settled near the Esiphongweni area where the Babambeni people of Chief Dakamela lived. Apparently, Makuni then moved to Ezinyangeni ,which at that time was located on the Harare Road near where the Insiza Railway Station now stands. Here the soil was rich and supported good grazing; the climate was cool. But under Chief Duha Mloyi, the Ezinyangeni people were evicted and resettled at present day Ezinyangeni at Nkayi. The Ezinyangeni now fell under the

---

[10] Family tree of Mathambo Ndlovu and Chief Sivalo provided by Mahlangu (Mrs Elizabeth Mzilethi) and Welshman Mabhena.
[11] Now Inkosikazi Communal Land
[12] Professor Solomon Nkiwane, both of whose grandfathers served Queen Lozikeyi, pers. comm
[13] Clarke and Nyathi, p.267. Rees's grandson Dr Ioan Bowen Rees gave us the date from family records. Perhaps Welshman did not know it. *"Guide to Heroes' Acre"* states that he was born in 1924. But Rev. Bowen Rees never returned to Matabeleland after 1919. (*The Guide* is called "Heroes' Acre" from now onwards).

jurisdiction of the Nkalakatha Ndiweni chieftainship under the Ojingeni ibutho.[14]

In 1915, Makuni Mabhena started the LMS church at Izihawu. He also became LMS minister at the new Zinyangeni. When Makuni's wife, MaNkomo, daughter of Mzaca, gave birth to their third and youngest son, the proud father asked Bowen Rees to baptise the infant and give him Rees's own name. Rees, a modest and shy man, agreed to baptise the child, but said he should be called, not Bowen, but Welshman.

Makuni Mabhena was not only a churchman; he was also an *inyanga* or traditional healer. He was, additionally, active in the public domain. In the late 1920's, he was a supporter of the Industrial and Commercial Workers' Union[15]. In the late 1940's, Makuni was a prominent supporter of the Matabele Home Society.[16]So baby Welshman was born into a tradition of heroes faithful to their king, public activists and progressive London Missionary Society Christians. These were principles by which Welshman would live his whole life.

CHILDHOOD AND SCHOOLING

While the Ndebele ruled their country, they lived in a compact area on a cool, fertile, well- watered open plateau. As white men occupied the best land, Ndebele élite households immediately felt the shortage of pasture, because they owned many cattle. Chief Sihuluhulu Mabhena and Chief Sivalo Mahlangu were two of the first chiefs to move their cattle and homes from the Ndebele

---

[14] Thanks to Pathisa Nyathi for this information from his obituary of Welshman Mabhena.

[15] The South African ICU, founded in 1919, became the central voice for African economic and political protest in the early 1920's. Masotsha Ndlovu founded the Southern Rhodesian ICU.

[16] Prince Nyamande Khumalo demanded a consolidated tract of land for his father, King Lobhengula's, people.

heartland to the "dark forests" of what are now called Nkayi and Lupane districts, but which the white settlers called the Shangani Reserve.[17] Chief Sivalo moved even before 1910. He moved very reluctantly: "We still don't like it here," he said at a chiefs' meeting in 1993. The move north had many disadvantages, but it did enable the Mabhenas to keep their cattle herds.[18]

So when the time came for young Welshman to herd the Mabhena family's animals, he did so at Ezinyangeni with his relative Peter Mahlangu, grandson of Queen Lozikeyi's chaplain, Mathambo Ndlovu. Welshman attended Zinyangeni Primary School from Sub-Standard A to Standard Three.

INYATHI, TIGER KLOOF, INYATHI, HIGHFIELDS AND BACK TO EZINYANGENI

In about 1938[19] Welshman proceeded to the primary school at Inyathi Mission, where he did Standards 4 to 6. From Inyathi,Welshman was selected to go to Tiger Kloof.

"Welshman had a passion for music," said his brother Norman. "He particularly loved church music."And music was very important in the struggle for freedom: songs were created for particular occasions, as a means of building morale. At Tiger Kloof Welshman composed a song called "Isitimela" (the train).

At Tiger Kloof, Welshman learned to be a skilled leatherworker making modern shoes. After qualifying he returned in 1948 to teach at Inyathi, which then offered industrial subjects. [20]

---

[17] Nkayi Chiefs' meeting, 26.8.1993
[18] Timon Mabhena and Norman Mabhena.
[19] The date was provided by Welshman's mother's sister's son John Robert Mzimela, who was at Inyathi School at the same time.
[20] Norman Mabhena.

"Maybe he was bonded (to work with the LMS)," said his cousin and classmate Mr John Robert Mzimela. "He had one year's break." Welshman now came to know Robert Mugabe[21]who was then teaching at Hope Fountain, another LMS school.[22] The two men used to play tennis at Inyathi.[23]

While teaching at Inyathi, Welshman met and fell in love with the beautiful Rebecca Dlodlo, daughter of Nhlanhla who was born to Tshotsha, the twin brother of Muntuwani Dlodlo of the Enqameni ibutho. Nhlanhla, who left Enqameni to live with his sister Queen Lozikeyi, was named Mazha, the Nyai equivalent of Nhlanhla. So Rebecca Dlodlo was the niece of Queen Lozikeyi Dlodlo.

MaDlodlo had attended Hope Fountain Primary School. There her teachers had included (briefly) Robert Mugabe and Tennyson Hlabangana. When MaDlodlo was introduced to Welshman, she was a temporary teacher at Hauke. They first saw each other at a teachers' meeting at Bulawayo.

Peter Mahlangu's brother-in-law Rev Amos Mzilethi[24] married Welshman Mabhena and Rebecca Dlodlo on 30th April 1950 at the LMS church at Hauke on what had been Queen Lozikeyi's ranch. Rebecca later trained as a nurse at Mount Selinda[25].

"I went to work at Zinyangeni Clinic when there were no more jobs for temporary teachers," said Mrs Mabhena.[26] She left her children to study at Mount Selinda. Mrs Mabhena's nursing qualification enabled her to support her family during the many years when Welshman could not do so.

---

[21] Later Zimbabwe's prime minister and president.
[22] Phillip Ndlovu, interview with Pathisa Nyathi.
[23] Pathisa Nyathi, pers. comm
[24] Amos Mzilethi married Elizabeth Mahlangu (previously married to a Mr Ncube).
[25] Mount Selinda is a mission near Chipinge. It developed into an important centre comprising a hospital and nurse training, school and teacher training..
[26] Mrs Mabhena.

Jeremiah Khabo was working at Inyathi School when Welshman taught there. The two men and their girlfriends were preparing for marriage at the same time. MaDlodlo told us that she remembered that her future husband could compose and write classical music.[27]

Jeremiah Khabo said: "Welshman had a choir at Inyathi. He made up a song called MaGumede, about the pickup van that was used to raid skokiaan (illicit brew) queens. Welshman would talk about the African National Congress of South Africa, for example with his brother-in-law Elkan Ndlovu, who was an ANC activist".[28]

Asked whether Welshman was influenced by the South African A. N.C. when he was at Tiger Kloof, Welshman's cousin John Robert Mzimela replied: "Everyone who left Matabeleland and went to South Africa got inspiration from the South African A.N.C. "

Welshman Mabhena was one of several Southern Rhodesians who returned to their own country ideologically armed to turn their own country into a battlefield, as Pathisa Nyathi wrote.[29]

Welshman cut his political teeth when he defied the unwritten rule that blacks were to crumple their hats as a sign of deference to the Native Commissioner. The ever-defiant Welshman challenged the native assistants and demanded to speak to the Native Commissioner in English. After all, he was a product of Tiger Kloof. Following this episode, some educated black people were treated with moderation.

Jeremiah Khabo remembered: "On one occasion Welshman was locked up for refusing to take off his hat for the Native Commissioner, Mr Cockcroft. This had an amusing sequel after Independence when Welshman and I were talking about this incident in Bulawayo, and I pointed out to Mabhena that Cockcroft, 'your old enemy', was nearby".

---

[27] Mrs Rebecca Mabhena, Garreth Mahlangu and a Mabhena grandson.
[28] Jeremiah Khabo, pers. comm.
[29] Nyathi Pathisa: *Lest we forget: George Silundika* (no publisher 2013) page 9

Many years later, Welshman told Oxford researchers: "My politics has just been a continuation of my father's work for the people."He returned to Inyathi School at the time when the parents of many of its students were being evicted from fertile Bubi District into the dark forests of the Shangani Reserve. The students' essays on their return from holiday were all about malaria and the death of cattle.[30] The white headmaster thought that it was Welshman rather than the experience of eviction that underlay these subversive writings.

When industrial subjects were phased out at Inyathi, Welshman moved with his family to Highfield in Salisbury (now Harare).They lived near Leopold Takawira who was headmaster of the school. Welshman went from school to school, teaching music.

At one time, Welshman worked for Cuthberts, a shoe company in Bulawayo. When he had accumulated enough capital, he decided to set up his own business at his rural home at Zinyangeni. He bought a machine on which he made shoes, handbags, belts and suitcases. At about this time, his father Makuni passed on.

Welshman soon became involved in a struggle for African people to claim land. South of Nkayi in Bubi District lay the extensive white-owned Kenilworth Estates. The owners, ever hungry for more land, extended the boundaries of the estate beyond the Guwe River. This angered the local people who were short of pasture for their animals. The Africans decided to approach the native commissioner: Welshman was one of four men appointed for this onerous task. The four men were arrested and served three months in jail. For Welshman, this was a taste of more incarceration to follow. While he and his colleagues were serving their prison terms, the local people continued to cut the Kenilworth fences till the white authorities

---

[30] The evictees from the Ndebele heartland lost up to half of their herds from the poisonous plant *umkhawuzane*, disease and wild animals when the evictees were forced to move into the Shangani Reserve, Alexander, McGregor and Ranger,p93. District Administrator Jack Nhliziyo recorded a heart breaking video account of his own family's eviction from Matabeleland South to Nkayii in 1952. Contact Mafela Trust.

decided that two paddocks should be ceded to nearby Gwiji and Guwe.[31]

THE EZINYANGENI NATIONALISTS [32]

A man attending Welshman Mabhena's funeral correctly remarked that he had helped kindle the fires of nationalism at Nkayi (and Silobela). In 1957 the Southern Rhodesian African National Congress (SRANC) was re-founded under Joshua Nkomo, and demanded independence: Welshman joined the SRANC.
Welshman worked in the 1950's and 60's with men such as Isaac Ronald Mswelaboya Sibanda, a member of the National Executive of the SRANC. Ronald Sibanda had come to Ezinyangeni as a teacher and was secretary of the local branch that Welshman chaired. Both men saw themselves as pre-eminently Ndebele. Both were modernisers and entrepreneurs. Maluzo Ndlovu was another close colleague of Welshman at Nkayi.

When the SRANC was banned in February 1959, Welshman invited the aged radical, Masotsha Ndlovu –who had been an activist with the ICU, the proto-nationalist Voice[33] and the SRANC- to come to speak at Ezinyangeni as an inspiration to younger people. The National Democratic Party (NDP) was founded on 1stJanuary 1960 and Welshman joined immediately.

"The formation of the NDP marked the beginning of a new era in search of the best African identity. There was increased African consciousness. .. The South African African National Congress

---

[31] For much of this information I am indebted to Mr Pathisa Nyathi's obituary of Welshman Mabhena.
[32] For the background to this section see Alexander, McGregor and Ranger pp 102 onwards.
[33] Benjamin Burombo in 1947 formed The British African Workers' Voice Association in Southern Rhodesia to unify Africans politically and fight for their better economic opportunities and social advancement.

anthem *'Nkosi sikelel'i- Afrika'* was adopted," wrote Pathisa Nyathi. [34] 1960 was called "the year of Africa" because so many African countries, formerly under various colonial masters, achieved independence.

"Welshman Mabhena was the person who brought me into this politics", said J Z Mzilethi, speaking about the period 1961-2.Three decades later Mr Mzilethi served as Provincial Administrator to Welshman Mabhena.

"Mabhena and I were related. I would sit on the back of his ZAPU scooter and he would take us all round Nkayi," said Mr Mzilethi. "He was a very good door-to-door organiser and I would listen to him talking to the elders. In some cases, I remember his talking about the government forcing the people to live in lines and letting the people talk about how bitter they were about this."

Dumiso Dabengwa, later chief of military intelligence of ZIPRA, first met Welshman at this time. "The struggle for him was about fighting colonialism," said Dabengwa. "But he wanted to make sure that Ndebele culture was preserved."

Women were also active in the Liberation Struggle and were inspired by Welshman. Obadiah Moyo,of the Rural Libraries and Resources Development Programme, told us that his mother, Laster Mpofu, was a political activist under the leadership of Mawelishi. In the 1930's, when Laster was a baby, the Mpofu family had been forcibly removed from fertile land in Bubi District close to the famous and holy Mwali Religious centre at the Mambo Hills (Intaba zikaMambo).The Mpofu family were dumped at Guwe in the Shangani Reserve in thick forest about 10 km south of Zinyangeni. The area was infested with tsetse flies.

Laster Mpofu was bitten and contracted sleeping sickness from which she suffered till her death in 2000. Her son Obadiah Moyo told us: "This colonial history and the brutality of the Rhodesian government on the local people fuelled my mother's hatred of this

---

[34]Nyathi, Pathisa: *Lest we forget: George Silundika,* p 18

regime. In Welshman Mabhena, my mother found a leader of the resistance movement that fought any laws introduced by this regime. On a number of occasions my mother was found by the Rhodesian police on the wrong side of the law."

By May 1961 Welshman was the co-ordinator and "super-efficient secretary" of a vigorous cluster of NDP branches in Nkayi District.[35]

The attempted enforcement of the Land Husbandry Act (1954) gave the NDP a target for non-co-operation and sabotage. The Act was basically a cattle culling measure and played straight into the hands of the nationalists. The ordinary peasants from then onwards tended to identify with the nationalist cause.

Laster Mpofu was one of the activists. "In the 1950's- 60's, when all families were asked to dip their cattle and take their children for immunisation injections against childhood diseases, my mother resisted such moves," said her son Obadiah Moyo. She mobilised other youths and heaped sand in dip-tanks and prevented mothers taking their children for immunisation."

Mr Moyo explained how he came to contract poliomyelitis in 1959, when he was three years old. Laster Mpofu had been convinced by Obadiah's grandmother that baby Obadiah should be taken for vaccination. "But my mother got wind that the police were hunting for her and as a result she abandoned the visit."

In short, Obadiah said, "Welshman Mabhena became the torch bearer for resistance and political activism in the whole region of Matabeleland and beyond. "

The result was described by the Native Commissioner, Nkayi:

"The efficient administration of the district was attacked from almost every angle, amongst which forms of attack the following might be noted-handing in of dip cards, blockage of dips, refusal to

---

[35] Interview with Welshman Mabhena recorded in Alexander, McGregor and Ranger, p 103

dip, widespread illegal meetings, boycott of cattle sales, mass refusal to pay personal and arrear native tax, mass refusal to be vaccinated and tuberculosis tested, ploughing at will in allocated areas, and general intimidation throughout the district, making the work of the police in detection and bringing to book extremely difficult." The Ezinyangeni activists had stimulated a populist movement.

There was increasing violence from the white minority regime. As early as September 1961, the NDP wrote to Prime Minister Edgar Whitehead protesting against "the reign of terror perpetrated by the police" at Nkayi. But two more plane loads of police were flown into the district to join those already on the ground. "The troubles are said to have spread to every part of the District," reported *The Daily News*.

The NDP was banned on December 9th 1961. Soldiers and police poured into Nkayi, taxes were collected at gunpoint. At the end of December, Joshua Nkomo publicly protested that the army had been flogging people at Nkayi.[36]

When the Zimbabwe African People's Union (ZAPU) emerged on 17 December 1961, Welshman joined immediately. [37]

In 1962, sabotage intensified. The Ezinyangeni nationalists, closely watched and harassed as they were by the representatives of the white regime, remained the best able to speak out. Welshman's colleague Ronald Sibanda led a ZAPU delegation to meet with the Minister of "Native Affairs." But the Minister and the Chief Native Commissioner spent most of the meeting abusing the delegation.

In 1962, ZAPU, led by Joshua Nkomo, decided to fight for the people's freedom.[38] In September of that year, the white minority regime gave the Nkayi police their head. Prosecutions began. At the

---

[36] Alexander, McGregor and Ranger, p 105
[37] "Heroes' Acre" page 261
[38] Nkomo, Zephaniah and Ndlovu, Sijabuliswe: The decision to take up arms: ZPRA's Untold Story (Mafela Trust, Bulawayo 2010).

end of the month, six restriction orders were served on ZAPU officials, including Welshman Mabhena who was restricted to Essexvale, (now Esigodini) in Matabeleland South, where "he had neither home nor relatives."

The nationalist movement had armed men from 1957. At first the weapons would mostly be home-made small arms to make petrol bombs. Welshman was an administrator, and part of the struggle was to infiltrate the white-led army, which also infiltrated ZAPU.[39]

Welshman had been arrested at Nkayi in 1963 while driving a car. He was accused of moving weapons. Probably the car was one of Ramanbhai K. Naik's vehicles. "One of the contributions I made to the struggle was transport," the Bulawayo- based Asian businessman told Marieke Clarke[40]. "Dumiso Dabengwa crossed the border to Zambia in my vehicle...I lost three cars to the Movement; the whites destroyed them....."

Welshman Mabhena later said of Ramanbhai: "R.K. was part of us in our struggle. He had an open hand. We did not have a single car or a bank account before we got in contact with, and got help from, the Asians. R.K. was one of those who briefed us, gave us other material benefits. Because he's here, he feels he's one of us...."[41]

Twenty five trucks came to the Mabhena house. [42]The trucks that came to the four-roomed Mabhena home at Zinyangeni were carrying many police and soldiers. There could have been more than 70. Some came into the house and some stayed outside. Welshman and his wife were alone. In the process the police started searching the house and may have found the box which contained Mrs

---

[39] Mafela Trust information.
[40] Pers comm to Marieke Clarke
[41] Welshman Mabhena, pers. comm.
[42] Mrs Mabhena told us the story of the house search.

Mabhena's sewing. One of the police may have put dynamite into that sewing box. Welshman was sent to prison for five years.

Welshman would be held in restriction areas and prisons until 1979, with only two weeks of freedom. Obadiah Moyo remembers his mother Laster Mpofu whispering to family members about the arrest of Mawelishi and what their response should be.

The harassment and imprisonment of leaders like Welshman Mabhena did not stop the development of the nationalist movement in the Shangani Reserve. Jocelyn Alexander, JoAnn McGregor and Terence Ranger wrote, following their research in the mid 1990's: "In moving through the districts of Lupane and Nkayi it was difficult to find adults who, at some time in their past, had not been politically active. ZAPU membership reached into every family if not every home. "[43]

WELSHMAN AND REBECCA'S CHILDREN

Welshman and Rebecca Mabhena had five children. The first born, Lindelwe, was a son; the other four were daughters: in birth order, Landiso, Thokozile, Ontibile and Nozipho. The boy and one girl have passed on. Welshman's commitment to the national cause was such that, Mrs Mabhena said, "Nozipho was nine months old and at the breast when Welshman went to detention. She had completed Form Four when he returned home." The burden of parenting as well as earning a living fell almost entirely on the mother.

When Welshman was in detention or held, Rebecca stayed at Nkayi, nursing at the Zinyangeni Clinic. Rebecca even ploughed the land, though in Matabeleland this heavy work was traditionally done by men. The children were at school at Mzilikazi Township in Bulawayo staying with family. Rebecca and Welshman already had the house at Four Winds.

---

[43] Alexander, McGregor and Ranger, *Violence and memory* page 3.

WELSHMAN MABHENA 1963-1979

Someone who came to know Welshman well towards the end of his life said: "He spent almost all his life dedicated to the freedom of this country and its people. He believed that others so involved felt the same way... Even when he was in prison, he believed that they were together" (united ideologically in the struggle.) "Throughout that period he had no time to attend to his personal or family life, or educate his children, let alone amass wealth like his colleagues. "

Welshman himself wrote[44]: "When "(in 1963)" I was taken from the High Court in Bulawayo to serve my five year sentence in Salisbury, my main concern was for my family. I felt buried alive and asked God to help my wife and young children. Surprisingly, I received a letter from my church minister which had not been opened by the prison censors. He advised me that if I wanted to retain my marriage I must be sure to use my bi-weekly writing privilege, and I made sure that every paper I was given was sent to(my wife). And when she wrote to me, she always tried to encourage me with news, and never complaining about problems.

"In prison I was busy studying. I finished my Matric and proceeded with Accounting."

Welshman passed Advanced Level and the Fellowship of the Association of Certified Bookkeepers of South Africa. He also attained a Bachelor of Commerce degree with the University of South Africa."[45]

"I didn't want to find myself left behind others when I came out of prison," he later wrote." I was sharing a cell with other political prisoners, some from ZAPU and others from ZANU, but I was the only Ndebele there. I learned to be very careful of tribalism. But we were very hopeful that we would be successful in our nationalist struggle. "

---

[44] The extended quotations by Mr Mabhena are from "Conscience be my guide" edited by Geoffrey Bould (Weaver Press, Harare, 2005)
[45] "Heroes Acre" page 262

While he was in Salisbury, Welshman "shared jail time" with Robert Mugabe.[46]

Welshman later wrote: "As soon as I was released "(in 1968)" after serving my term I went to my home area."

Much had happened while he was in jail. In 1963, ZANU broke away from ZAPU, which led to on-going and extreme antagonism between the two parties. The hated Federation of Rhodesia and Nyasaland was dissolved on 31 December 1963. Malawi and Zambia became independent the next year. A white minority government under Ian Smith declared Unilateral Declaration of Independence (UDI) of Rhodesia on 11th November 1965. But still the British colonial masters did not bring majority rule to Rhodesia (now Zimbabwe).

In early April 1966, a group of eight ZAPU guerrillas set out from Zambia and entered Matabeleland. They were not the first armed men[47]to be sent into the country. But these combatants were the first to enter the country on foot and interact with the civilian population. For three whole months the guerrillas lived inside Rhodesia, with one group sent to Tsholotsho in preparation for the 1967 Wankie Campaign (the Luthuli Detachment).This was a joint military operation involving ZAPU and Umkhonto we Sizwe, the military wing of the African National Congress of South Africa.

Phiillip Ndlovu was a freedom fighter with the ZIPRA[48] forces under ZAPU led by Joshua Nkomo. "So I had.. known about Welshman Mabhena alongside other ZAPU politicians and nationalists such as Sydney Malunga, Edward Ndlovu and several others."[49]

The white minority regime was determined to hold on to power. Atrocities committed by the regime in these years included the

---

[46] Later Zimbabwe's prime minister and president.
[47] Women in the ZAPU forces did not go into battle
[48] ZIPRA was founded in 1971.
[49] Interview by Pathisa Nyathi with Mr P. Ndlovu

22

deliberate spread of anthrax spores to cattle and people, including probably at Nkayi.

"Enormous numbers of cattle died," said Patricia Battye[50], "and some people died up country. Reginald Austin[51]confirmed to me recently that the anthrax was indeed deliberately spread from the Andrew Fleming Hospital[52] in Salisbury by the white government. A clinic at Hyde Park treated the 'endless cases'of anthrax brought in from Matabeleland North over many months," said Ms Battye.

WELSHMAN MABHENA IN GONAKUDZINGWA

After only two weeks of freedom in 1968, Welshman was re-arrested.

Norman Mabhena suggested that his brother was rearrested because the release of such a popular figure caused such great excitement and raised morale among African people that the white minority regime decided to lock him up again.[53]

Welshman remained inside until just before Zimbabwe's Independence. First he was sent to Wha Wha..." "Then I was taken to Gonakudzingwa, under indefinite restriction. There were several camps which were full of ZAPU activists. Most were released as the years passed and finally we remained as only seven, right up until 1979.... We organised ourselves, trying to protect ourselves against infiltration and maintain discipline and morale. We felt we were still participating in the struggle. We knew what was happening outside, often being told by the police who guarded us. I was the spokesman for our group and the experience of articulating our issues to the police helped us later. When some comrades were released, we would smuggle out messages with them, written with lemon juice

---

[50] A social worker for 30 years in Bulawayo's townships. Marieke Clarke recorded her story in England.
[51] A distinguished Bulawayo-born lawyer of international fame who worked with ZAPU.
[52] Now the Parirenyatwa Hospital. (Pathisa Nyathi.)
[53] Norman Mabhena

and hidden inside the heels of their shoes. Of course it was discouraging when so many left and we were just a few remaining behind; sometimes we felt we were studying just for the sake of it and we would never come out. It was our families who gave us support by keeping strong for us.

"Our treatment was not so bad, partly because Amnesty International (AI) and the International Committee of the Red Cross (ICRC)[54] each came twice a year to check on the conditions and made sure that we were well treated. One time the Ghanaian Dr J.B. (Danquah)[55] came with the Red Cross. He had been imprisoned and tortured by (Kwame) Nkrumah and he warned us that, once we were free, we would find our own people doing the same to us. And indeed it happened to me."[56]

Mrs Mabhena and the children were sometimes allowed to visit Welshman when he was in prison or at WhaWha.[57]In the late 1960's, Laster Mpofu, Obadiah Moyo's mother, stayed with her cousins the Siso family at Zinyangeni, assisting them with household chores. The Sisos were neighbours to the Mabhenas. Both Mr and Mrs Siso were teachers at Zinyangeni Primary School. So, little Obadiah met Mrs Mabhena. "Welshman Mabhena was in detention and his wife MaDlodlo had just returned from visiting him. In a whispering voice, MaDlodlo gave Mrs Siso, my mother and other women gathered together a briefing on how Mawelishi was doing and what he expected of them. As children, we were chased away and never allowed to be close to where such whispering was taking place."

---

[54] But the ICRC was withdrawn after UDI in 1965

[55] Dr Joseph B. Danquah (1895-1965) was a Ghanaian political leader and a principal founder of the Gold Coast nationalist movement. In 1960 he decided to run for President against Nkrumah. Danquah received only 10% of the vote. He was imprisoned in 1961 under the Preventive Detention Act. Released in 1962 and elected President of the Ghana Bar Association, he was again imprisoned early in 1964 and died a year later in prison. *Various internet sources.*

[56] Bould, Geoffrey (ed) *Conscience be my guide*

[57] Mrs Mabhena, pers.comm

Welshman's example led Laster Mpofu to choose his old school when it was time for her son to have secondary education. "When it was time for me to seek a secondary school place in 1972, my mother said that my first choice should be Inyathi Mission, the school where Welshman Mabhena went for his education. Luckily I got a place."

Obadiah Moyo continued: "Later my own political baptism came when as students (at Inyathi School) we started to research more about the Liberation Struggle and the men and women behind it. My mother's activism, the leadership of Welshman Mabhena, and the political awareness of the Shangani people, all this I shared with other students at Inyathi Mission.

"A lot of us were from the rural areas and we understood the oppression that our own parents were going through and the tilling in barren lands. Armed with tools of education we saw ourselves as liberators of our parents, who sold their cattle to ensure that we had a good education. Such was the influence of Welshman Mabhena, to my mother, to me and finally to my politically alert fellow students.

"Welshman Mabhena being from the Shangani Reserve and a former student of Inyathi Mission became one of our heroes and role model. The discussions motivated us and gave hope that indeed the struggle for a free nation will one day be a reality. This made us work hard in our studies- with the hope that one day we shall be leaders in a free Zimbabwe. Many students left, either soon after Form Four or in the middle of their studies, to join the Liberation Struggle, and ZIPRA, the military wing of ZAPU, the political party of Mawelishi, was their destiny."

INDEPENDENCE, 1980

Zimbabwe's War of Liberation cost perhaps 50,000 lives.[58]Negotiations at Lancaster House in London and a ceasefire on 21 December 1979 led to rushed elections in February 1980, and a peace settlement. The hurried process was due to American pressure on Britain, exerted to pre-empt further Soviet and Cuban involvement in Zimbabwe. ZANU-PF led by Robert Mugabe won the elections,[59] and became Prime Minister. Rev. Canaan Banana became Zimbabwe's first president.

Welshman Mabhena was released at the time of the Lancaster House Talks. "When he was released, he went straight back into politics," said his wife.[60]

But Welshman Mabhena did not forget people who had cared for his wife when he was unable to do so. Obadiah Moyo told us: "On a number of occasions, after Independence, Welshman Mabhena would thank the Siso family, especially Mrs Siso, and women like my mother and others, for taking good care of his wife MaDlodlo when he was in prison and detention."

1980 was a time of optimism as well as of on-going insecurity and violence in Zimbabwe. Everywhere suspicious guerrillas had to turn themselves in to Assembly Points, long -secretive political cadres had to come into the open, order had to be consolidated and elections held.

Jack P. Nhliziyo, who later became District Administrator at several postings in Matabeleland North, and whose home is at Nkayi, came to know Welshman Mabhena at this time. "I got to know (him) at Independence when he was trying to gather ex-combatants into Assembly Points (APs). In our area, the AP was at St Paul's. (Welshman) and others, travelling in ZAPU military cars, would

---

[58] Chitiyo, Knox, pers comm.
[59] Scarnecchia, Timothy Rationalizing Gukurahundi: Cold War and South African Foreign Relations with Zimbabwe 1981-3 (Kronos Volume 37, No 1)

[60] Mrs Mabhena, Garreth Mahlangu and a Mabhena grandson.

travel up and down gathering in ex-freedom fighters. He and others would convince them that they had to come to the APs."[61]

At Independence, Welshman became a district councillor at Nkayi and was elected chairman by the other members.[62] "Someone of Welshman's eminence could have expected to become an MP," said Mr Nhliziyo. But the first elections after Independence were fought on a party list system.

"Joshua Nkomo imposed as the Nkayi MP Vote Moyo, who was from Matabeleland South and an ally of Nkomo... I don't think that Welshman and Nkomo saw eye to eye," said Mr Nhliziyo.

Mr Nhliziyo pointed out that Amos Mkhwananzi, the other key Matabeleland North ZAPU personality, was also excluded from parliament in 1980. Mr Mkhwananzi became the first chair of the Tsholotsho District Council. It seems that Joshua Nkomo wanted to fit his allies into parliament and took advantage of the opportunities he had to place people.[63]

Phillip Ndlovu, later Chief Executive Officer of Nkayi District Council, said "Welshman was convinced Nkomo went out of his way to sideline him." Welshman was a forthright man who did not attempt to conceal his views and feelings on certain issues. [64]

A regional authority for Matabeleland North and South was soon established and Welshman became chairman. This Regional Authority, aimed to monitor (centrally directed) development progress, proved to be too big. It was narrowed down to two Provincial Authorities, one each for Matabeleland North and Matabeleland South.

Following Independence, there were particular challenges facing regions loyal to ZAPU.

---

[61] Nhliziyo, Jack, interviewed by Pathisa Nyathi
[62] Nhliziyo, Jack.
[63] Jack Nhliziyo, interviewed by Pathisa Nyathi
[64]Phillip Ndlovu's Interview with Pathisa Nyathi.

"When ZAPU lost the 1980 elections to ZANU, the Ndebele people were perceived to be a political threat," said Pathisa Nyathi[65]. "The fear of economic marginalisation drove a wedge between the Ndebele and the Shona."

The escalation of violence after the end of the Liberation War built on the two guerrilla armies' regional patterns of recruitment and operation during the 1970's, and the history of animosity and distrust (greatly encouraged by the white minority regime) between the two nationalist armies and their political leaders. These patterns had left ZIPRA forces dominated by Ndebele speakers while ZANLA was predominantly Shona speaking.

Robert Mugabe had dealt ruthlessly with opposition throughout his career.[66]He was also determined to have a one-party state in Zimbabwe. The Cold War offered him and ZANU-PF the international "cover" to carry out atrocities against civilians in western and central Zimbabwe so as to destroy the ZAPU political leadership of that region.

In late 1980, Prime Minister Mugabe and President Kim II Sung of North Korea signed a treaty of friendship. Within that agreement lay the seeds of what was to emerge as the Fifth Brigade, answerable only to Mugabe. North Korea would train and arm the Fifth Brigade for the Zimbabwean government.

Prime Minister Mugabe, who had appointed Joshua Nkomo to the important portfolio of Home Affairs, demoted him in January 1981 to the portfolio of Minister for the Public Service, and then demoted him again to Minister without Portfolio. Nkomo had put his views on a one-party state to 40,000 supporters at Bulawayo's White City Stadium on 1st June 1980. He said a one-party state was an ideal

[65] Speaking at Oxford at BZS Research Day 2014
[66] Ranger, Terence reported in Association of Concerned Africa Scholars Review 89 Spring 2015; page 47

situation, but that it must not be introduced without the unanimous agreement of Zimbabwe's entire population. [67]

In October 1981, Prime Minister Mugabe toured Zimbabwe emphasising his belief in the urgent necessity of a one-party state. An astute observer then heard someone in Bulawayo laugh and say: "Why doesn't he come here, say he wants a one-party state and see what reception he gets?"

Then immediately the person became serious and said, "But if he comes and gets a bad reception, then we won't get any land."[68]There was all-pervading anxiety about the Fifth Brigade.[69]

In February 1982, Mr Mugabe announced that arms caches had been found on ZAPU properties. Troops were moved onto all holdings associated with that party. The discovery of the caches led to the breakdown of the fragile ruling coalition. On 17th February, Mugabe sacked Dr Nkomo and most other ZAPU members from his cabinet. [70]The timing of the attacks on ZAPU must also be understood as part of a larger competition over economic resources between the two political parties and their guerrilla forces. ZAPU would suffer greatly as Mugabe and his colleagues began to claim ZAPU properties. [71]

The apartheid South African government had been shocked by ZANU's victory in the 1980 elections. This drove South Africa back onto bringing about violence and subversion in neighbouring countries. One example was that South Africa supplied a small amount of weapons to ZIPRA dissidents. (The former ZIPRA fighters called "Super ZAPU" who became dissidents never numbered more than 400.)The apartheid state also trained and

---

[67] Todd, Judith Garfield, *Through the Darkness* (Zebra Press, Cape Town, South Africa 2007) page 35
[68] Todd, Judith, ibid, *page 35*
[69] Todd ibid, page 36..
[70] Todd, ibid, page 43.
[71] Sibanda, Eliakim, *The Zimbabwe African People's Union 1961-1987* (Trenton, NJ, Africa World Press 2003)

armed a small number [72](the so-called "Super ZAPU")of Zimbabwean insurgents. ZANU-PF was able to stigmatise the disaffected ZIPRA combatants as stooges of the apartheid state.[73]The "Super ZAPU" had better weapons and more ammunition than the former ZIPRA fighters.

Soon the people of Nkayi and Lupane districts[74]were collectively subjected to extreme violence as supporters of ZAPU.

On 29th January 1983, at the full meeting of councillors of Lupane, the District Administrator announced the arrival of the Fifth Brigade, warning that the Brigade had power to punish and kill without having to report to the police or any civilian administration. The councillors were told that the purpose of this exercise was to eradicate "dissidents." A German medical doctor, Johanna F. Davis, resident and working at Nkayi and Lupane since the late 1940's, told the army commander that she considered the people living there to be as law-abiding and peace-loving as anywhere in the country. Her views were ignored.

The almost entirely Shona-speaking Fifth Brigade, numbering between 2500 and 3500 mainly former ZANLA fighters[75], launched what Dr Davis called a "wide-ranging reign of terror in Matabeleland and the Midlands." [76]The doctor witnessed the atrocities at first hand but stayed at her post throughout the military campaign, known as Gukurahundi.

Gukurahundi began in January 1983 and then returned before, during and after the 1985 general elections. Political and development activities were completely paralysed. During and after the Fifth Brigade's depredations, the Central Intelligence

---

[72] Never more than 100
[73] Onslow, Sue, *South Africa and Zimbabwean Independence*, in Onslow, ed, *Cold War in Southern Africa*
[74] The modern names for the areas formerly called the Shangani Reserve.
[75] Scarnecchia, page 92
[76] For Dr Davis's observations, see her autobiography, *Mission Accomplished*, published in Bulawayo, 2013.

Organisation (CIO) and ZANU (PF) Youth carried out a more targeted programme of political violence.[77]This happened although, apart from the 400 ZAPU dissidents and the 100 South African-supported Super ZAPU, there was very little in the way of direct military resistance to the Fifth Brigade.[78]

Welshman Mabhena was a vocal critic of Gukurahundi, said one of his former local government officers, as was Amos Mkhwananzi of Tsholotsho.

"Early in 1983, Welshman was still chair of the Nkayi District Council, but failing to organise council meetings. He sought refuge in Bulawayo,"[79]said Mr Jack Nhliziyo. Gukurahundi may have cost the lives of 20,000 to 30,000 men, women and children in Western Zimbabwe.[80]

Prime Minister Mugabe had said of Joshua Nkomo: "ZAPU and its leader, Dr Joshua Nkomo, are like a cobra in the house. The only way to deal effectively with a snake is to strike and destroy its head".

In early March 1983, police sealed off the high density suburbs of Bulawayo, in one of which, Pelandaba, Joshua Nkomo had built his home. Within the police cordon, Fifth Brigade soldiers searched for Dr Nkomo, but were unable to find him. Soon he received a message that his driver and two others had been shot dead in cold blood at his house. The killers then rampaged through his home, destroying all they could.[81] Nkomo left the country, crossing the border to Botswana. He returned to Zimbabwe later in the year.

Professor Timothy Scarnecchia remarks : "Given the realities of the Gukurahundi against the backdrop of the Cold War and South

---

[77] Alexander, McGregor and Ranger, page 224
[78] Scarnecchia, page 102
[79] Nhliziyo pers. comm.
[80] Background information by Scarnecchia. Figures of victims suggested by Dr Knox Chitiyo to MC, June 2015.
[81] Todd ibid, p 57

Africa's regional strategy, the Ndebele were virtually 'friendless', while ZANU-PF managed to obtain the support of '(Western powers)', the '(Soviet Union)', and to a certain extent even South Africa, so long as ZANU-PF and the Fifth Brigade continued to target ZAPU, ZIPRA and by extension the ability of the African National Congress of South Africa to operate in Zimbabwe."

In answer to the question: "Gukurahundi took place at the time Welshman was at Nkayi. What was his role?" Mr Phillip Ndlovu, later Chief Executive Officer at Nkayi District Council, answered: "Those were difficult times and Welshman stood by his people. When the onslaught intensified in the more remote corners of the district, he advised the people to come to the Nkayi Centre in small numbers, preferably in ones, in order not to attract the prying eyes of the government agents and (Fifth Brigade). But people were coming in their thousands to seek refuge. "[82]

According to Welshman's nephew Timon, Welshman went during Gukurahundi to Prime Minister Robert Mugabe and asked, "Why are you killing my people?" [83]

Welshman and Rebecca Mabhena had a beautiful home at Zinyangeni, but this was destroyed by ZANU (PF) youths: only the concrete base remains.

"When the Fifth Brigade, the Red Berets, were at Nkayi," said Mrs Mabhena, "ZANU-PF youth in the District Development Fund (DDF) vehicles came to the Mabhena home and burned it down."[84]

"All the family's clothes, crockery, *amacansi* (floor mats) were taken, then burned," a former local government officer told Marieke Clarke.[85]"Then the cattle were killed. The ZANU-PF people had two targets: Welshman and the Nkayi District Administrator, Mr

---

[82] Interview of Phillip Ndlovu with Pathisa Nyathi
[83] Pers comm to MC
[84] Mrs Mabhena, pers comm.
[85] Interview in England.

Godfrey S. Maphosa. From Welshman and Rebecca Mabhena's's ruined house, the ZANU-PF people went to the District Administrator's home. Godfrey S. Maphosa was taken out of this house, beaten to a pulp and left for dead. Mr Maphosa's office workers then looked for him and smuggled him into Bulawayo."

Very fortunately, by chance, during Gukurahundi, Mrs Mabhena was asked to attend a month's course at Mpilo Hospital in Bulawayo. She left a herd boy and a grandson at home.

"Nkayi had a very bad time during Gukurahundi, just because of Welshman," she said. Mrs Hleziphi Dlodlo[86] warned Mrs Mabhena, while she was at Mpilo Hospital, never to go back to Zinyangeni "or the Fifth Brigade would do anything they wanted to her."[87]

"I had no home," said Mrs Mabhena. She told the nursing instructors at Mpilo Hospital, and the Bulawayo City Council found her a place at Pelandaba Township. She worked at Khami Clinic till she retired.

In later years, Welshman is reported to have said, "The heroes are the people who were buried in the police camps"- the victims of Gukurahundi.

WELSHMAN AS MP AT NKAYI

The second general elections after Independence were held on 1st and 2nd July 1985. These were Zimbabwe's first single-member constituency-based elections. ZAPU won every seat in Matabeleland and was returned with an overwhelming majority in both Nkayi and

---

[86]MaNcube, who by 2013 was the Nkayi District Administrator.
[87] Mrs Mabhena pers. comm.

Lupane Districts. Welshman now became MP for Nkayi with 25,874 votes to ZANU(PF)'s 760 and UANC's 366[88].

But ZAPU's organisational base and leadership were greatly weakened by the events of the two previous years. The repression effectively denied the people of Matabeleland a voice in development.

Welshman was an outspoken critic of those that stifled development in Nkayi. "He was keen to see other people develop and yet he was emasculated and incapacitated to do so," said Phillip Ndlovu[89].

Mr Phillip Ndlovu said:

"As a member of parliament he was part of the legislative arm of government but was not in charge of anything. He did not control resources for the implementation of development projects in his constituency. He had a vision for the development of Nkayi, but faced immense frustration when he could not avail the requisite resources as he was not in charge. For example, he was interested in developing Duha Mzondo School, but could do pretty little to advance the school, in which he had personal interest. He even suggested to Council officials like us to move building material from elsewhere in order to facilitate the construction of the school of his heart. As Council our hands were tied by procedure. .. That became a source of frustration for Welshman".

When Phillip Ndlovu applied for the post of Chief Executive Officer at Nkayi Rural District Council, a job that he started in 1988, Welshman was on the interviewing panel. With Stanley Bhebhe, the District Administrator, Welshman was instrumental in the decision to appoint Mr Ndlovu, who "was being stifled by the ZANU-PF people" in another area.

At Nkayi, Mr Ndlovu said: "I discovered that Welshman was a great lover of his people. He remained in touch with the people and kept a

---

[88] Alexander, McGregor and Ranger, p 227.
[89] Interview with Pathisa Nyathi

pulse on his followers. He undertook frequent visits to the communities. He sat down with the people and engaged them in close developmental and political discussions with a view to identifying their needs. I could describe Welshman Mabhena as a man of the people, a shepherd who knew his flock intimately."[90]

"Welshman used to say to his constituents, 'This is your thing' (development issues).' It is not mine. I am just like a fish which requires water in order for it to survive. I am the fish and you are the water. I need you, you need me. We need each other.' The man was so close to the electorate that there was no way you could beat him when it came to elections. He was development-orientated and really wanted to serve his people."

Mr Ndlovu continued: "Welshman regarded the petrol filling station as a meeting place for the people in the Nkayi Constituency who visited him there. Several meetings were held at the filling station... That constant interaction and interfacing with the ordinary folk helped him keep a pulse on community needs and aspirations."[91]

WELSHMAN MABHENA BECOMES ZAPU SECRETARY-GENERAL

At the 1985 ZAPU Congress, John Nkomo was elected Secretary-General. Joshua Nkomo was not happy, as the party might appear to be an Nkomo party with Joshua Nkomo and John Nkomo in top positions. Two names were then put forward, those of Cephas Msipa and Welshman Mabhena. Welshman was elected Secretary-General. This meant that he was "one of the most powerful people around Nkomo, and a hard-liner," said a former local government officer. "Welshman never opted for soft things. He always took the most difficult path."

Just after the 1985 elections, "There were dissidents running all over the place," said the then Matabeleland North Provincial

[90] Interview of Mr Phillip Ndlovu by Pathisa Nyathi, 22nd August 2014.
[91] Pathisa Nyathi: Interview with Phillip Ndlovu

Administrator J Z Mzilethi, who started his job in September of that year. "But because of the development that we implemented, they did not try to kill me. They had the confidence that I would not say things against them. In fact there were two groups of dissidents: the real ones, and plants. I handpicked my District Administrators."

The late Oxford University Professor, Terence Ranger, remarked that his research in Zimbabwe in the 1990's (some of which Welshman Mabhena facilitated, see below) intensified Ranger's disillusionment with the results of the victorious nationalist movement: "The earlier aspirations for plural democracy and human rights had been replaced by a ruthless one-party majoritarianism, ready to repress any opposition", wrote Ranger. [92]

"ZANU-PF was keen to poach Welshman to their side," said Phillip Ndlovu." Always principled and choosing to be with his people, Welshman turned down the frequent advances. Deserting his people at their greatest hour of need was tantamount to selling out," said Mr Ndlovu. "He was strongly loyal to ZAPU and no amount of coercion, persuasion or cajoling could sway him. He was as steadfast as rock. "

Only a few weeks after the elections, in August 1985, Welshman, with two other ZAPU members of parliament, was arrested. Welshman "enjoyed his freedom but never Independence," remarked the highly experienced local government officer Jack Nhliziyo.

One answer to the question "Why was Welshman arrested then?" was that ZANU-PF wanted to punish ZAPU for its success in the recent elections. The aim was to weaken the party as Prime Minister Mugabe strove to introduce a one-party state.

---

[92] In 2003 the University of Zimbabwe published Prof Ranger's edited collection, which traced the development within the nationalist movement from emancipation to totalitarianism. Ranger reported in *Association of Concerned Africa Scholars Review 89, Spring 2015*, page 46.

A retired senior local government officer said that Welshman was locked up at this point because he was ZAPU Secretary-General and highly critical of Gukurahundi. Welshman was detained at Eiffel Flats police station from 1985-6[93]. Here he suffered under the Kadoma-based Central Intelligence Organisation (CIO) official Ernest Tekere.

"I was... accused of plotting to overthrow the ZANU-PF government, something I would never do," Welshman wrote later. "For a whole week I was tortured, someone standing on my legs and hitting the soles of my feet with a pick handle. They wanted me to admit that I was plotting against the government and were trying to get me to implicate Joshua Nkomo. But they couldn't break me. Imprisonment under ZANU (PF) was horrible –much worse than under (Ian) Smith[94], but we survived just because we knew that the State was trying to break us and we wouldn't accept that.

"But even while in the police cells, there was something useful I could do. The police compound was behind our cells, and at night I could hear women screaming while they were being beaten by their husbands. Sometimes I would see a woman going away with her children. Then I called the police officers and told them to stop mistreating their wives, threatening to report them to the Officer-in-Charge...

"My hope was that there were people in parliament who would speak out and we could be released. Finally, I was brought to Chikurubi Maximum Security Prison in Harare while they were preparing us for the trial. When the case was withdrawn, they just dumped us in the streets in our prison uniform: probably they wanted to shoot us and say we were escaping from prison. But our lawyer forced them to release us properly..."[95]

---

[93] Eiffel Flats is a village seven km east of Kadoma.
[94] Prime Minister of Southern Rhodesia from 1964.
[95] This extended quote is taken from Bould, Geoffrey, *Conscience be my guide*, page 53/4

When Welshman was released from prison, he was working as a shoemaker and "doing politics" said his nephew Timon Mabhena.

THE UNITY ACCORD

Early in September 1985, President Canaan Banana invited Joshua Nkomo to meet at State House in Harare to discuss the unification of PF- ZAPU and ZANU (PF). Dr Nkomo must have concluded that there was no other way to stop the violence and repression being inflicted by Prime Minister Mugabe through his party, except to succumb[96].

Well-informed contacts in Matabeleland said that the Prime Minister was compelled to negotiate for a Unity Accord. He was under international pressure and he had nearly manoeuvred himself into a position where he was caught between two hostile forces, Renamo in Mozambique and ZAPU. Offers were coming of military help for Joshua Nkomo, probably from Eastern Europe.

Former Provincial Administrator for Matabeleland North J Z Mzilethi told us that Welshman played a crucial role in bringing about the Unity Accord. "He travelled all over the country asking people to join the Unity Process," he said."When they came together, they could develop the country."

The Unity Accord of December 1987 led to the merger of ZANU(PF) and PF-ZAPU under the name ZANU(PF) and finally brought peace to Matabeleland.

In the negotiations, the centre of dispute was the unified party's name. The composition of a unified leadership, ideology and policy were all less important than the name of the unified party. Joshua Nkomo argued that it would be difficult to convince his supporters to accept an unmodified name, that it would leave ZAPU with no recognition of its lengthy history. But ZAPU was forced to concede.

---

[96] Todd, ibid, page 109

In 1987 Robert Mugabe became President of Zimbabwe and Joshua Nkomo was made ceremonial Vice-President. Welshman Mabhena was appointed Deputy Minister of Political Affairs and elected Deputy Speaker of Parliament. He also became ZANU-PF Matabeleland North Provincial Chairman. In 1992 he was made Governor of Matabeleland North.

"Welshman thought that things would be sorted out after the Unity Accord," said a retired local government officer." That's when he joined ZANU-PF, as a way to unify the nation."

But Welshman's cousin and former schoolmate Mr J R Mzimela was not convinced: "I walked out of the Unity Accord meetings," he said. "I disagreed with the Patriotic Front name."[97]

ZANU(PF)'s leaders expected Unity to open the way for a one-party state. Instead, it brought a flowering of political dissent. The contradictions inherent in Unity were expressed in a popular metaphor: that of marriage.

"We're still ZAPU in that marriage: a woman doesn't lose her (isibongo) maiden name even if she uses her husband's name".

WELSHMAN MABHENA AS GOVERNOR

Welshman Mabhena's judgement to support the Unity Agreement proved correct. When the present writer visited Matabeleland North in 1989, all her contacts thoroughly welcomed the Unity Accord as absolutely the only way forward. There was a strong feeling that now there would no longer be any excuse for the neglect of Matabeleland.

But Welshman Mabhena's power, when he became Governor in August 1992, was limited. The Five Year Plan had already been made. "Your role as governor was supposed to be to toe the line, to

---

[97] Mr Mzimela, pers. comm

implement the plan, and to do so 'correctly,'" said his brother Norman Mabhena.[98]

Dumiso Dabengwa said: "Welshman regretted that he was appointed governor by the president when he would have preferred to be elected by the people. If he had been elected by the people, he would have had loyalty to the people and not to the president".

Welshman's Provincial Administrator 1992-1994, J Z Mzilethi, added: "Welshman followed Lobhengula. There was a purpose in having provinces from 1980, to provide decentralisation and devolution. (Welshman) worked closely with the chiefs. Because he was of noble background, they listened to him. Welshman Mabhena believed in the sons of the soil, local leaders, taking responsibility for the areas devolved to them. Traditional dances and Ndebele culture, for instance, should be maintained."[99]

"Welshman did not differentiate between people according to their party," said his nephew Timon Mabhena." He had a common vision for the people of Matabeleland and he would speak his mind… He was a very approachable governor. Anyone could walk into his office. He would never refuse to see anyone. He had no sense of fear. He used to assist across tribal lines."[100]

"Welshman spoke his mind, right or wrong. He expressed his opinion the way his heart dictated to him," remarked another informant. "Welshman was strongly committed to the development of Matabeleland and spoke out openly about anyone trying to stop the people from self- determination. He very much believed in devolution."

About the same time that Welshman was appointed Governor of Matabeleland North, Ernest Tekere, formerly of the CIO at Eiffel Flats in Kadoma, was promoted to head the CIO in Bulawayo, where he had to report to Governor Mabhena. Welshman, among others,

---

[98] Pers comm
[99] Mr Mzilethi pers. comm
[100] Timon Mabhena, pers comm.

had suffered under Tekere during his detention at Eiffel Flats. When Judith Todd heard of their new relationship, she asked Welshman, "How can you bear it?"

She wrote:[101] "Governor Mabhena looked at me with a still, steady, delighted grin. After a few seconds he answered my question with another: 'Shouldn't you be asking, how can *he* bear it?'"

The present writer commented years later to former Provincial Administrator J Z Mzilethi on the great and well-directed development that she saw happening from 1989 into the 1990's. Mr Mzilethi replied "That development took place because of our own sweat, and Mabhena was instrumental in it... I enjoyed working with Welshman. ."

It was obvious when I returned in 1989 after 25 years to Matabeleland that people in Bubi District, where I had previously taught, were expressing their confidence following the Unity Agreement. They had a trusted Provincial Administrator (J Z Mzilethi) and District Administrator (Jack P Nhliziyo) who had both studied at Inyathi School. These were their own people and highly regarded. As house guest of the District Administrator, I toured for a week and a half in February 1989 all over Bubi District. We drove many miles safely along the so-called Fighting Road that the white settler regime had built as a kind of firewall against freedom fighters. I reported at the time:(Provincial Administrator) "J.Z. Mzilethi is using his power and influence to support and develop the spirit of confidence which has sprung up among local people since the Unity Agreement."[102]

---

[101] In Todd, ibid, page 114
[102] Clarke, Marieke, "Inyathi revisited"; paper presented to Professor Terence Ranger's seminar, 1989

WELSHMAN MABHENA AND LAND REFORM:

Support for the people of Inyathi Communal Land as they claim the land

Zimbabwe's freedom struggle was fuelled by the determination to win back the land that had been violently occupied by white men. Land reform was a matter of urgent concern to almost every Ndebele. While the Africans ruled their country, they lived in a compact area on a cool, fertile, well- watered open plateau. Bubi District was part of the fertile heartland of Matabeleland. White men had been trying to grab it ever since the invasions in the 1890's. Almost every Ndebele household had been evicted from their original homes so that white farmers could farm the land. We have seen Welshman Mabhena as a young man trying to stop white men extending the Kenilworth Estates in Bubi District.

We have seen how Laster Mpofu's nationalism was fuelled by her family's eviction from that District in the 1930's. Another evictee among many more from Bubi District was the future Provincial Administrator J. Zwelibanzi Mzilethi. He and his family had to leave their home in 1942, because a white man wanted their land.[103]

Welshman Mabhena had strong views on land reform. According to Dumiso Dabengwa, Welshman wanted the distribution of land to take into consideration the origin of the people, lest the Ndebele culture end up being diluted. He said that people to be settled on any (ex -white men's) farms acquired by government should be local people, not settlers brought in from outside.

During my visit to Inyathi in 1989, I learned that the former London Missionary Society Farm had been resettled. The new owners (no longer local people who were mission tenants) were by no means all local people. This was the kind of resettlement that Welshman regarded as inappropriate. He also disapproved of central government policy change concerning land reform: the law was

---

[103] Jack Nhliziyo, pers. comm

changed to support land grabs, which could cause chaos as well as injustice.

Under the white settler regime, three small areas of Bubi District had been "reserved" as "Communal Lands" for Africans who could no longer live in their old homes.[104] One was the ranch of Queen Lozikeyi, from which she had refused to move.[105]It is now Inkosikazi Communal Land. A second Communal Land, that at Inyathi, was tiny, potentially fertile but grossly overgrazed.[106]In 1989 this had six thousand people and 1000 cattle in 11 square miles. The human population was about 760 per square km.[107]One in twelve households was landless. White men's farms hemmed in the Inyathi Communal Landon all sides. Though Inyathi Communal Land people did encroach on properties that stood in the name of local white farmers, the Africans had to wait several decades for their land hunger to be assuaged.

Even at the height of the Liberation War, the Ndebele had mostly refrained from attacking the white farmers who occupied their former land. The Ndebele living nearby found it hard to regard them as enemies.[108]In fact only seven commercial ranchers were killed on their land during the liberation war in the whole of Matabeleland. [109]

Welshman Mabhena did what he could to promote land reform after he became Governor of Matabeleland North in 1992. He wrote to the white farmers of the province to ask them to justify how they could each own several huge properties. The answers were very revealing. George Parkin, for instance, referring to his vast estates,

---

[104] The Reserves were renamed "Communal Lands" after Independence.
[105] See Clarke and Nyathi, page 229
[106] The third was at Intabazinduna.
[107] The population density of the highly fertile delta, the Netherlands, was reportedly (only) about 407 per square km in 2015 (latest available figures). This figure is given to show how overcrowded the Inyathi CL was.
[108] Pers comm at Inyathi, 1989.
[109] Alexander, Jocelyn, *The Unsettled Land*, page 4, quoting Collet Nkala in *Parade*, April 1989, page 43

said 'I want them all'. In the end, he lost them all, by forced acquisition.[110]

By 1989, however, considerable areas of land in Matabeleland North were slowly being moved from white to black control.[111]Welshman Mabhena was directly involved in the following case.

Shortly after Independence, when the "willing seller, willing buyer" policy was introduced, Mr Jeremiah Khabo (who had taught with Welshman at Inyathi School) started discussing with Mike Huckle, the son of an elderly widowed woman farmer, Mrs Huckle, whose land lay next to the Inyathi Communal Land. Mr Khabo has long been a natural leader of the Inyathi Communal Land people.

"I had known the Huckle family for many years," said Jeremiah Khabo. "When the Huckle parents played tennis, we African boys acted as paid ball boys... I started talking to the Huckles shortly after 1980. We had talked with Welshman Mabhena to the Huckles. "

In 1996, with Dr Ioan Bowen Rees, the grandson of Rev Bowen Rees, I made a social visit to Mrs Huckle. It was understood that, after Mrs Huckle's death, her land would be made available for Inyathi people to graze their cattle. And so it has come about.

"Our cattle can now go anywhere because, under government policy post 1980, local people can no longer be driven away as they used to be. When the old Mrs Huckle died, the fences were broken, the homestead was dilapidated. The Huckle sons had their own farms. Our cattle can now run anywhere, just what we wanted," said Mr Khabo in 2013.[112]

---

[110] Jeremiah Khabo, pers comm to MC.
[111] The present writer noted these in detail in her paper "Inyathi revisited" at an Oxford seminar in 1989.
[112] Pers comm to MC

Having Welshman Mabhena as provincial governor, a man who fully understood local people's issues helped in a quiet way peacefully to redistribute some land in the manner that best suited the Inyathi people's needs.

WELSHMAN MABHENA AND DEVELOPMENT PROJECTS IN MATABELELAND NORTH

Most informants stressed that Welshman's dreams for Matabeleland North met much resistance from central government in Harare. One example was the construction of a tarred road from Bulawayo to Nkayi. Welshman initiated the construction of this road. There was very valuable timber at Nkayi and Lupane: having a tarred road would make it possible efficiently to extract the timber. The wood was much used to sustain the Bulawayo timber and building industries, which employed thousands of people. But "Enemies of ZAPU", informants said, "obstructed that road."

"This road was one classic example of Welshman's frustrations," said Phillip Ndlovu in 2014." There was literally no progress. As we speak, the road has not reached Inyathi Mission, after all those years." (He was right. I had a fairly rough journey to Inyathi from Bulawayo in October 2015). "ZANU is not in the habit of advancing the fortunes of one it perceives as an enemy... "[113]

Another great disappointment was the failure to implement the Matabeleland Zambezi Water Project, which would go far to solve Bulawayo's chronic water problems.

"Right up to his death, Welshman Mabhena protested loudly at what he saw as a deliberate ZANU PF government policy to

---

[113] Interview with Pathisa Nyathi, August 2014.

"marginalise" Matabeleland by prioritising development projects for other provinces."[114]

GOVERNOR WELSHMAN MABHENA AS A CHAMPION OF EDUCATION AND LITERACY

Welshman Mabhena "was a modern traditionalist," his former Provincial Administrator J.Z. Mzilethi told us."He loved and was interested in everything to do with education and seeing people being educated, to liberate their minds and physically ensure that the people got the education they needed. He loved the Ndebele language. He was a very passionate politician. Welshman Mabhena said that development had to be practical and he saw it from the educational point of view."

Welshman's Provincial Administrator J Z Mzilethi said: "What Mabhena used to complain about was that there were no institutions in Matabeleland led by an Ndebele. When Welshman Mabhena was Governor, the President's control over state institutions included the placing of Shona speakers in charge of even the first year of education.[115] As a result, small children were not learning their mother tongue from native speakers. Mabhena would criticise this policy and strongly oppose it."

"In schools it was compulsory to teach Shona. What Mabhena thought was that the language policy should be as it was under the whites: Zulu or Ndebele to be the language taught in Matabeleland and Shona in Mashonaland. English should be the national language... "[116]

---

[114] an obituary with the bye-line New Zimbabwe in www. zimdiaspora.com/index
[115] Much of this paragraph derives from information from Norman Mabhena
[116] Mr Mzilethi, pers. comm

"The law stated that a young child should be educated in his or her own language," said Timon Mabhena. "When Welshman stood up and said so, he was called a tribalist. There was an outcry. David Coltart[117] has now implemented this policy and nobody could say that Coltart was a tribalist."[118]

Welshman would talk about the underdevelopment of Matabeleland compared to other regions. Teachers were appointed by the Public Service Commission and not by the head teacher. Mabhena thought that Ndebele children with better qualifications were held back from studying in Mashonaland. He did not hesitate to speak out on this issue.[119] Welshman "teamed up with the then mayor of Bulawayo, Joshua Malinga, to call for the enrolment of local children in local government institutions."[120]

Welshman Mabhena, a former teacher turned politician, advocated for education and literacy facilities being made accessible to all Zimbabweans, especially those in rural areas, Obadiah Moyo told us.

Realising the limited number of schools and lack of libraries in the rural areas, Mabhena called for the building of new schools and expansion of existing ones. As a Member of Parliament for Nkayi District and later as Governor for Matabeleland North Province, he encouraged Rural District Councils to construct more schools to reduce the distance that children had to walk to schools.

We have seen above from the testimony of Phillip Ndlovu how Mabhena as MP tried to build a new school at Duha Mzondo, and the problems he faced. But nonetheless he was able, as early as 1980,

---

[117] Minister for Education, Sport, Arts and Culture from February 2009 until August 2013.
[118] Interview with Timon Mabhena at Bulawayo, 2013
[119] Norman Mabhena, pers comm.
[120] Pathisa Nyathi: obituary of Welshman Mabhena.

as chair of the provincial authority, to found two important development institutions, namely Hlangabeza at Nkayi and Tsholotsho High School. "He was aware of and "would have loved" the Quaker Rural Training Centre at Hlekweni in Matabeleland South[121]" said his former Provincial Administrator. "Mabhena would say 'If this chap is failing at school, send him to Andrew Ndiweni at Hlekweni.'"

So, early in his career as a local government official, Welshman showed his enthusiasm for education, which was a passion all his life. He always questioned why communities in the Matabeleland region were being marginalised by the government when it came to provision of adequate education infrastructure, thus leading to their low pass rates, we were told.

His intervention saw the number of schools in each district in Matabeleland North Province increasing by at least 30%, during the time he was Governor. New secondary schools, opening new doors for scholars graduating from primary schools were built, each absorbing children from at least three feeder primary schools.

"Rural libraries were at the heart of Welshman Mabhena", said Obadiah Moyo,"and he officiated at the opening of a couple of such libraries falling under the auspices of the Rural Libraries and Resources Development Programme (RLRDP)."

Welshman's wish to preserve Ndebele culture was strong and well known. The idea to commemorate Mzilikazi Day was hatched in his office and the first celebrations were held in 2000. The present writer attended the celebrations in Bulawayo and also, twice, in London.

Welshman had also evidently thought a lot about education. A former local government officer said that in 1991/2 she accompanied

---

[121] Founded in 1967

Welshman to a school at Komayanga." It had a very useful link with a UK school. Welshman gave a very moving speech", she said, "about tolerance, diversity, openness to new ideas, leadership at local level and not just leadership from government to government. I thought this was one of his best speeches."

WELSHMAN AND FREEDOM OF INFORMATION

After Welshman Mabhena became Governor, three historians from the UK[122] recorded the memories of the people of the Nkayi and Lupane districts. The historians had his total support. The local government officers working for him opened their archives so that the historians had a complete administrative record from 1897 to 1985. The three were the first researchers able to make full use of the official correspondence of independent Zimbabwe.

So Welshman Mabhena, ignoring the convention that 30 years must pass before state archives are opened, made a big contribution to freedom of information in his country. The book that was published using the research is called "Violence and Memory" and was published in 2000.

The distinguished human rights activist, Shari Eppel, told us that "Human rights work was easier in Matabeleland in the 1990s. Such work was facilitated by the ZAPU old guard within ZANU, of which Welshman Mabhena was one."

WELSHMAN MABHENA, REBECCA DLODLO MABHENA AND THE STORY OF QUEEN LOZIKEYI

---

[122] Jocelyn Alexander, JoAnn McGregor and Terence Ranger

During a visit to Nkayi in the early 1990's, the present writer asked Mr and Mrs Mabhena if it might be possible to write the biography of Queen Lozikeyi Dlodlo. District Administrator Jack Nhliziyo had explained the importance of the great queen.

The setting for the first long conversation with Mr and Mrs Mabhena was extraordinary. We were lunching at what had been the white settlers' club at Nkayi. The windows had been inserted into the building above the height of a man's head so as to protect the whites inside if freedom fighters attacked the building. Now the white settlers were long gone and the present writer, the only white person present, the house guest of District Administrator Jack Nhliziyo, was munching isitshwala and beef, sitting next to Governor and Mrs Mabhena.

I seized the opportunity. Queen Lozikeyi was the elder sister of Mrs Mabhena's father Mazha Dlodlo. "Would you allow me to write the biography of Queen Lozikeyi?" I asked.

The Mabhenas not only gave permission, they did everything they could to help me and Pathisa Nyathi with the research.

The Governor and MaDlodlo made introductions, sent interviewees to see me and Mr Nyathi. The Mabhenas arranged at least one visit. On one occasion the Governor actually interpreted, as the queen's former personal assistant, MaTshuma, spoke about her long deceased royal mistress[123]. MaTshuma gave me crucial evidence about the critical battle at the Mambo Hills in July 1896. Though many white men wrote their version of the story of that desperately sad encounter, it took a black woman speaking through the Governor of independent Zimbabwe's Matabeleland North province to reveal the words of black women sheltering in the caves of the doomed stronghold.

---

[123] The queen died in the influenza epidemic in 1919. MaTshuma died shortly before the book on her mistress was launched at Bulawayo in 2010.

White men in Matabeleland in the 1890's were infamous for their sexual misconduct with black women[124]. To the white soldiers shooting indiscriminately at unarmed civilians, the women in the Mambo Hills caves had yelled: "Don't you want a fuck?" (The aristocratic and gentlemanly Welshman, a staunch Christian, struggled to find the obscene expression. The British visitors supplied the word.) "And the white men stopped their deadly assault,"[125]MaTshuma told us. Not only the great queen Lozikeyi but ordinary black women had outwitted white men armed with guns.

Welshman Mabhena, a son-in-law of the Dlodlo family that provided King Lobhengula's senior queen, for the first time revealed to a British historian some of Queen Lozikeyi's strategies that enabled her to outwit, awe and almost defeat her white opponents. It was Welshman who called Queen Lozikeyi the "Oliver Tambo" of the Ndebele, because she, like the famous South African A.N.C. leader, kept her people together after a disaster. [126]So, for the first time, the great queen's role in co-ordinating the 1896 Revolt was made public.[127]

Welshman was a warm and generous friend. In 1996 he and his wife entertained me and Dr and Mrs Ioan Bowen Rees for a night at the Mabhena farm, on commercial farm land. In this way the links between the missionary Bowen Rees and the present generation could be nourished.

---

[124] For evidence see Clarke and Nyathi, especially Chapter Four.
[125] The story of the Mambo Hills battle is told in Clarke and Nyathi, Chapter Five.
[126] See especially Chapters Four and Six of Clarke and Nyathi
[127] Terence Ranger published "Revolt in Southern Rhodesia", a beautifully researched and rightly famous book in 1967. But he did not mention Queen Lozikeyi's leading role, just because the Ndebele people were not in the 1960's willing to reveal her importance to the outside world. The Unity Accord and the agreement of the Dlodlo family were needed before the truth could be published.

Right up to the end of his life, with a strong sense of history, Welshman Mabhena was aware of British government duplicity with regard to Matabeleland.[128] In 2007 he wrote a stinging letter to the British ambassador to Zimbabwe advocating an autonomous Matabeleland State. He called it a "notice of intent to file an application for the review of the verdict of the Judicial Committee of the Privy Council in the Land Case Matabeleland of 1918".

The letter said "Your Excellency, you may be surprised that I usually get lost when I come across people who mix up my country Matabeleland with Zimbabwe, because Zimbabwe is a former British colony which was colonised in 1890 and granted independence on 18 April 1980.

"My homeland Matabeleland, on the other hand, is a territory which was an independent Kingdom until it was invaded by the British South Africa Company on 4th November 1893 in defiance of Her Majesty Queen Victoria.

"Actually in terms of the Moffat Treaty of Peace and Unity of 11 February 1888 between Queen Victoria and King Lobhengula, Britain and Matabeleland were allies and, due to our respect for our late king, we have not renounced his vow."

WELSHMAN MABHENA: TOWARDS DISMISSAL

"Welshman is best remembered for his fearlessness," wrote Pathisa Nyathi. "He never wavered from speaking out on the marginalisation of Matabeleland."

"To Welshman, a 'No' was a 'no' and could not deviate from a stated position. When he chose to stand by you, you could bank on

---

[128] For some historical background see Clarke and Nyathi, especially Chapter Three

him," said Phillip Ndlovu. "As a result, Welshman became a marked man, one who was stripped of all political power by the ZANU (PF) people. At one time they even wanted to take away his house in the township. Under pressure, Welshman phoned me at (Nkayi) Council and sought advice. He had forgotten the person who signed his forms at the time he acquired the house. Apparently I still remembered that it was the girl who worked for him at the petrol filling station. That was how he got back his house. His wife Rebecca phoned up to thank me for saving their house."[129]

In 1994, against Mabhena's wishes, his Provincial Administrator J. Zwelibanzi Mzilethi was transferred to Matabeleland South. Welshman "publicly cried at the party he was giving for my farewell because he did not want me to be transferred," said Mr Mzilethi. Welshman said to Mzilethi:" I want to work with you".[130]

(Morgan) "Tsvangirai wanted Welshman to join the Movement for Democratic Change (MDC)," said Mrs Mabhena. But Welshman refused.[131]

"In 2000 the Movement for Democratic Change won lots of seats, when Welshman was still in ZANU-PF, so as to be loyal to the Unity Accord," said Timon Mabhena."A Governor should be above party politics so he went to the MDC victory party. Soon after this" in August 2000" he was dismissed."[132]

"His tenure of office had not been renewed by the head of state....He was replaced by Obert Mpofu," said Mr Mzilethi.

"He was accused of not having campaigned hard enough for ZANU-PF", wrote Pathisa Nyathi. [133]According to a ZAPU spokesman, Mabhena had called on President Mugabe to resign and make way for younger people.

---

[129] Interview of Pathisa Nyathi with Phillip Ndlovu.
[130] J Z Mzilethi, pers. comm
[131] Mrs Mabhena, pers comm..
[132] Timon Mabhena, pers.comm
[133] Obituary of Welshman Mabhena

WELSHMAN MABHENA, THE LAST YEARS

"Politics was engrained in Welshman." said one informant."He talked politics, he dreamed politics and he slept politics. He was a politician through and through. If I ever tried to divert him from politics to real life issues, he refused."This commitment may have been a cause of his disregard of conventional time, on which some contributors to this biography have remarked.

Someone who was close to Welshman in his last years thought that his commitment to politics had left him very vulnerable in old age. The Mabhenas' only son had died and the daughters were living far away outside Zimbabwe.

Welshman had criticised the new government policy permitting land grabs. "Welshman's farm was occupied by war veterans," a former local government officer said. "He disdained to negotiate with them, went to Harare and talked to President Mugabe. He refused to be pushed around by a bunch of thugs. President Mugabe phoned the war vets. And they left the ranch."

But a close friend said that "unlike the people who remained in power, Welshman had never built up wealth." He was "so unaware of his own rights" that he was not even a member of a medical aid scheme five years before his death. By that time he would have been 86 years old.

One of our informants tried to help the Mabhenas in old age by improving their herd and introducing modern cattle rearing methods. This friend painted a beautiful picture of the elderly Mabhenas at home: "Every weekend I would take Welshman and MaDlodlo to their farm. He felt so relaxed and refreshed whenever I took him out to the farm: he was so distressed. We would go to the cattle pens. I built a bench for him so he could sit there in the shade while I vaccinated the cattle. He loved it. ..."

WELSHMAN: DEVOTED TO CHURCH AND TO MUSIC TO THE END

Welshman attended church regularly, right up to his last days, said his brother Norman. He went to the UCCSA [134]church at Famona. Welshman loved the church. [135]

The distinguished Ndebele musician Albert Nyathi recorded his memories of Welshman in old age:

"Welshman was the main guest," he said, "at the launch of my last album. I knew him as a very kind old man. He was very passionate about the preservation of culture, about which he talked when I launched my album. He was worried that our culture was fast disappearing, our language getting diluted. He would speak of our dreams, aspirations and desires, with language expressing our emotions."[136]

WELSHMAN MABHENA: WHERE SHOULD HE BE BURIED?

Alvord Mabena asked Welshman where he and MaDlodlo wanted to be buried.

"We got the document" (with his stated wishes) "signed and handed it to lawyers. I negotiated with the City Council to locate a plot. .. Timon Mabhena and I built the graves (at Lady Stanley Cemetery, and had them watered. ... "[137]

Welshman Mabhena died at his home at Four Winds, Bulawayo, on 5th October 2010.

---

[134] The United Congregational Church of Southern Africa is the London Missionary Society's modern name.
[135] Norman Mabhena, pers comm
[136] Pers comm. Albert Nyathi
[137] Pers.comm to M.C. October 2013

Mr Phillip Ndlovu provided a fitting epitaph: "Once a comrade, always a comrade; so it was with Welshman Mabhena, a man of all seasons. A true son of the soil whose life he dedicated to serve his own people."

Pathisa Nyathi wrote:[138] "It was land appropriation that led national hero Welshman Mabhena to spend long periods of incarceration in Rhodesian prisons, making him one of the longest serving prisoners in the protracted struggle for independence. It was therefore only befitting that he be declared a national hero. He certainly deserved the honour. May your very dear soul rest in eternal peace."

The distinguished German missionary doctor Johanna F Davis, who had witnessed the full horrors of Gukurahundi at Lupane, and given medical assistance to many victims, said: "Welshman and I embraced the last time we met. I felt so sympathetic for what he suffered under the Smith regime and now too. They gave him a wonderful funeral."[139]

The funeral was held at the UCCSA Church at Njube in Bulawayo, which holds around 1000 people. Welshman had contributed to the building of that church. And "as we left the cemetery" said Welshman's brother Norman Mabhena, "cars were still coming in."

In a last talk to his former Provincial Administrator, J Z Mzilethi, Welshman Mabhena said, "Who will look after my people[140] when I am gone?" "He died fighting", said Mzilethi.

Obadiah Moyo, who knew Mawelishi when he was a political activist in the Shangani, wrote:

" The legacy of Mawelishi lives on and as young people read through the pages of this biography, more should see the need to contribute to a better Zimbabwe for All- -a dream we had at Inyathi Mission. "

---

138 In his obituary of Welshman Mabhena
139 Pers comm to Marieke Clarke, Bulawayo 2013.
140 He meant the people of Matabeleland.

ACKNOWLEDGEMENTS

INTERVIEWEES AND OTHER CONTRIBUTORS INCLUDED:

Welshman Mabhena; Mrs Rebecca Mabhena; Alvord Mabena; Norman Mabhena; Timon Mabhena; a Mabhena grandson; Garreth Mahlangu (representing Chief Sivalo); John Robert Mzimela; Dumiso Dabengwa; Jeremiah Khabo; Obadiah Moyo; J. Zwelibanzi Mzilethi; Phillip Ndlovu; Jack P. Nhliziyo; Albert Nyathi.

Sections were extracted from interviews or discussions with Patricia Battye, the late Dr Ioan Bowen Rees and the late Ramanbhai K. Naik. The final text was agreed by Mrs Mabhena, Norman Mabhena, Timon Mabhena, Marieke Clarke and Pathisa Nyathi.

BOOKS AND OTHER ACADEMIC WORKS CONSULTED OR USED

Alexander, Jocelyn; McGregor, JoAnn and Ranger, Terence: *Violence and Memory: 100 years in the Dark Forests of Matabeleland.* (James Currey, Heinemann, David Philip and Weaver Press,Harare 2000)

Bhebe, Ngwabi: *Benjamin Burombo* (The College Press, Harare,1989)

Bould, Geoffrey (editor): *Conscience be my Guide: An Anthology of Prison Writings* (Zed Press London and Weaver Press, Harare, 2005).Contains some of Mr Mabhena's prison memories. The copyright for these quotes was his.

Clarke, Marieke and Nyathi, Pathisa: *Lozikeyi Dlodlo, Queen of the Ndebele: 'A very dangerous and intriguing Woman'.* (Amagugu Publishers, Bulawayo 2010).

Raftopoulos, Brian and Phimister, Ian (eds) :*Keep on Knocking* (Baobab Books, Harare, 1997)

Scarnecchia, Timothy: *Rationalising Gukurahundi: Cold War and South African Foreign Relations with Zimbabwe,1981-1983.* (Kronos Volume 37, No 1)

Todd, Judith Garfield: *Through the Darkness: A Life in Zimbabwe.* (Zebra Press, South Africa,2007)

Welshman Mabhena before marriage

Mrs Rebecca Mabhena visiting her husband at Gonakudzingwa Restriction Camp. From left : John Ndlovu, Joel, Norman Mabhena, Mrs Mabhena, Welshman Mabhena, Abel Siwela, Misheck Whinya.

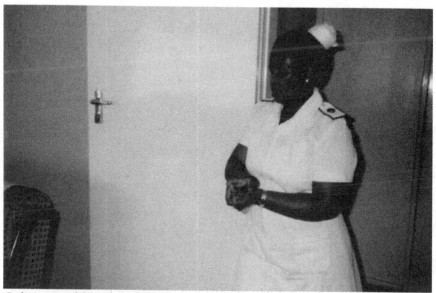

Rebecca Mabhena during training as a nurse at Mount Selinda. Welshman Mabhena was at Gonakudzingwa at the time.

Mabhena house at Zinyangeni on the occasion of Selebalo and Landiso's reception. The House was burnt down during Gukurahundi.

Welshman and Norman Mabhena at Gonakudzingwa, 1974

Welshman Mabhena at Nkayi (I am the fish, you are the water. We need each other)

From left: Norman Mabhena, Welshman Mabhena, Abel Siwela at
Gonakudzingwa in 1974

Welshman Mabhena at Mhlahlandlela Government Complex office as
Governor for Matabeleland North

Welshman Mabhena after being discharged from Mater Dei Hospital, taken on a visit to recuperate in the Matobo Hills.

Mr and Mrs Mabhena with their family.

Salukazana Nkomo, Welshman's mother with son- in-law Selebalo at the Mabhenas' house (F51) in Mzilikazi Township.

Mr and Mrs Welshman Mabhena
in August 2000 after being dropped as Governor for Matebeleland North.

Mr and Mrs Mabhena at their Amatja Road house in Fourwinds, Bulawayo

Dr Themba S. Dlodlo and Welshman Mabhena
Seated from left: Mrs Rebecca Mabhena and Dr Riita Dlodlo (MaGumede)

Nephews and nieces within a cattle pen at the Mabhenas' farm.

Mr and Mrs Mabhena, their cattle on the farm (1996)

Mr and Mrs Mabhena in their house on Matja Road, Fourwinds. Bulawayo
(picture by Jocelyn Alexander)

Ramnabhai Naik (left) ; Maganbhai (who drove him) : Don Naik at Oxford, 2008

Some members of the ZAPU national executive, Welshman Mabhena is third from the right

NATIONAL EXECUTIVE:

1.	Dr.J.N.M.Nkomo	President.
2.	J.W.Maika	Vice President.
3.	W.H.Mabhena	Secretary General.
4.	N.C.M.Nyashanu	Deputy Secretary General.
5.	K.M.Mano	Treasurer General.
6.	N.K.Ndlovu	National Chairman.
7.	R.G.Marango	National Organizing Secretary.
8.	J.L.Nkomo	Executive Secretary for Publicity and Inform.
9.	R.P.Nyandoro (Director)	Executive Secretary for Transport.
10	E#D.Ndlovu	Executive Secretary for Political Education.
11.	S.J.Nkomo	Executive Secretary for Foreign Affairs.
12.	N.Zikhali	Executive Secretary for Youth Affairs.
13.	Mrs.M.Makwavarara	Executive Secretary for Women Affairs.
14.	Dr.I.Nyathi	Executive Secretary for Security.
15.	Adv.S.K.M.Sibanda	Executive Secretary for Legal Affairs.
16.	Dr.K.L.Lube	Executive Secretary for Education.
17.	A.Masawi	Executive Secretary for Tradition and Culture.
18.	L.G.Madiye	Executive Secretary for Public Relations.
19.	M.Chinamasa	Executive Secretary for Commerce and Industry.
20.	Mrs.H.L.Chinamano	Executive Secretary for Welfare Services.
21.	Dr.S.U.Sakupwanya	Executive Secretary for Health Services.
22.	H.M.Bhebe	Executive Secretary for Mines.
23.	J.Padzakashamba	Executive Secretary for Construction.
24.	K.B.Bhebe (Director)	Executive Secretary for Agriculture.
25.	N.Moyo	Executive Secretary for Economic Plg and Devel

DEPUTY EXECUTIVE SECRETARIES:

26.	S.K.Vuma	Deputy Executive Treasurer General
27.	H.S.K.Mazendame	Vice National Chairman (Acting).
28.	S.D.Malunga	Deputy National Organizing Secretary.
29.	Mrs.A.Masuku	Deputy National Organizing Secretary.
30.	B.Hollington	Deputy National Organizing Secretary.
31.	P.Chilimanzi	Deputy Executive Secretary for Publicity and I
32.	W.Dhlamini	Deputy Executive Secretary for Transport
33.	D.Mangwende	Deputy Executive Secretary for Pol.Education.
34.	N.Mabhena	Deputy Executive Secretary for Foreign Affairs
35.	M.Chiranganyika	Deputy Executive Secretary for Youth Affairs.

36. W.Knife — Deputy Executive Secretary for Youth Affairs.
37. T.V.Lesabe — Deputy Executive Secretary for Women Affairs.
38. D.Dabengwa — Deputy Executive Secretary for Security.
39. Adv.S.Katsere — Deputy Executive Secretary for Legal Affairs.
40. Adv.L.Senda-Moyo — Deputy Executive Secretary for Legal Affairs.
41. Prof.G.P.Kahari — Deputy Executive Secretary for Education.
42. Chief J.M.Mangwende — Deputy Executive Secretary for Tradition & Culture.
43. K.C.Muhodi — Deputy Executive Secretary for Public Relations.
44. E.Khan — Deputy Executive Secretary for Commerce & Industry
45. Rev. Masiyane — Deputy Executive Secretary for Welfare Services.
46. E.D.Hananda (Director) — Deputy Executive Secretary for Health Services.
47. T.V.Mpofu — Deputy Executive Secretary for Mines.
48. F.Takundwa (Director) — Deputy Executive Secretary for Construction.
49. F.Matende — Deputy Executive Secretary for Agriculture.
50. S.D.Mhlongwa — Deputy Exective Secretary for Econ.Plu & Develop.

ADMINISTRATION:

51. S.Chatsama — Secretary for Administration.
52. B.Tshuma — Deputy Secretary for Administration.
53. J.Mafa — Deputy Secretary for Administration.
54. A.Njawaya — Financial Secretary in the Administration.

OTHER CENTRAL COMMITTEE MEMBERS:

55. M.Masiyakurima — Director
56. Skwili K.Moyo — Director
57. F.Matumbike — Director
58. A.G.Mkwananzi — Director
59. G.Mutazu
60. A.B.Nonye
61. A.Ndlovu.
62. S.Mabika.
63. P.Njini
64. Mrs.I.Murape.
65. Mrs.E.Mafu
66. Miss N.Ndlovu
67. Mrs.R.Mururi.
68. Mrs.Harare
69. Mrs.E.Nkiwane
70. K.Madzorera
71. Mrs.J.Mhindurwa

72. M.Muzvondiwa
73. Mrs. L.Ngwenya
74. A.T.Musongelwa
75. A.D.N.Tshabalala
76. S.Bhebe
77. Mrs.S.Mtoti
78. Mrs.J.Musingarabwi
79. S.Njini
80. R.Tshuma
81. F.Chipudla
82. V.H.Moyo
83. Mrs.Dhlamini (Y)
84. Z.Kanyasa
85. E.Hokonya
86. L.Mathuthu
87. D.R.S.Mamvutho.
88. S.K.Moyo
89. F.Mukombwe (MP)
9C J.Ngwenya
91. J.Dauramanzi
92. M. Machonisa
93. A.Tsuro
94. G.Gwenzi
95. E.Nyandoro
96. Chief V.Maduna
97. R.Ngugama
98. P.Mupanduki
99. Edward M.Chilimanzi
100. Adv.C.Ndebele.

101 E. MDHLONGWA
102 L DUBE (MN)

74

Printed in the United States
By Bookmasters